GOD
Is Always by
Your Side

GOD
Is Always by
Your Side

...a comforting reminder
that God is never
far away

A Blue Mountain Arts® Collection

Edited by Becky McKay

Blue Mountain Press™
Boulder, Colorado

Scripture quotation marked NIV is from THE HOLY BIBLE, NEW INTERNATIONAL VERSION®, NIV® Copyright © 1973, 1978, 1984, 2011 by Biblica, Inc.® Used by permission. All rights reserved worldwide. Scripture quotation marked AMP is taken from the Amplified® Bible. Copyright © 1954, 1958, 1962, 1964, 1965, 1987 by The Lockman Foundation. Used by permission. All rights reserved.

Library of Congress Control Number: 2014949901
ISBN: 978-1-59842-864-3

◪ and Blue Mountain Press are registered in U.S. Patent and Trademark Office. Certain trademarks are used under license.

Printed in China.
Second Printing: 2016

Blue Mountain Arts, Inc.
P.O. Box 4549, Boulder, Colorado 80306

Contents

God Will Take Care
of You

Someone's watching over you
   with the greatest love.
Someone wants you to be
   happy, safe, and secure.
Someone considers you
   a wonderful individual
   and cares about your needs.
Someone's making blessings
   for your benefit right now —
like sunshine for those rainy days
and rainbows to remind you
   of the promise up ahead.

Someone's watching over you always...
   and He will take good care of you.

— Barbara J. Hall

Trust God on Your Journey

Be open to what each day asks of you
and welcome what it may hold,
knowing the desires of your heart
    are in God's hands.
No matter where life leads,
He goes with you step by step
with open arms and heart;
trust Him on your journey.

He is the maker of every dream
and the keeper of all His promises;
share in the joy of celebrating
    what He's given you.
Find joy in every opportunity
to live out His purpose for you,
and know your efforts have meaning.
Accept any detours as part of His plan.
Keep your eyes on God,
and you'll never lose your way.

— Linda E. Knight

He Is in Control

Knowing God has a plan for your life is very important. When things happen that are out of your control, it can be very discouraging. It's easy to become frustrated, to feel afraid, and to question what the future holds. Putting your faith in God's plan allows you to trust that the events in your life are meant to be. It helps you to make choices that must be made and realize things are not really out of control — they are under His control.

There is a peace that can be found knowing that His plan is playing out in your life. When things are confusing for you, remember that God is in control and that He loves you.

— Rick Norman

God knows your every thought,
your every sorrow,
your deepest desire,
and your every need.

God never leaves you
where He found you.
He desires to show you
great and marvelous things through
patience, trust, and a willing heart.
If you just believe, He will lead the way,
unlocking what once seemed impossible.

God knows who He made you to be.
The good work He started in you
He will complete.
That is His promise.

Put this promise in your heart.
Reflect on it every day.
If something comes along
that makes you doubt,
remember the words written
on your heart.

God knows His plan for you —
a plan that will bring you happiness,
prosperity, and all the fulfillment
your heart desires.

You are blessed,
yesterday, today, and always.
God knows what He is doing,
even if sometimes
you don't understand.
He only asks that you trust in Him.

— Lisa Mae Huddleston

With Each Sunrise,
God Gives You
a New Beginning

One of God's greatest gifts
is the chance to be born again each day.
Beginning with every sunrise,
you can let go of the past
and any regrets, mistakes,
    or sorrows it may have held.
You can look ahead and see
    where you'd like to go,
secure in the knowledge that
God enables you to leave
    any emotional baggage
where it belongs — in the past.
You can choose to leave yesterday behind
and start over again today —
to be whoever and whatever
    you dream of being.
Know that with God's help
and His constant, loving attention,
you can achieve anything... beginning today.

— Edmund O'Neill

A Comforting Reminder

If you need to lean on someone,
   there is no greater strength.
If you need to move away from
   difficulty and toward resolve,
      there is no greater direction to go in.
If you wish to walk with happiness,
   there is no greater
   traveling companion…

God will be there for you.

If you are filled with questions,
    there is no better place to look
    for the answers.
If you are troubled, there is no
    refuge more safe and secure.
If you wish to reach for a star,
    there are no words of encouragement
    greater than His are.
If you seek serenity, understanding,
    and joy, then follow your heart
    when it tells you to believe.

For God will be there for you.

— Alin Austin

God Has Given Us
So Many Wonderful
Blessings

God gave us the seasons —
　　each with its own beauty and reason,
　　　　each meant to bring us a blessing,
　　　　　　a joy, and a feeling of love.
God gave us dreams —
　　each with its own secret,
　　　　each sent to give us feelings of
　　　　　　inspiration, hope, and tranquility.
God gave us the sunshine,
　　the rainbows and the rain,
　　　　the beauty and freedom of nature
to teach us the wisdom of gentle acceptance…

God gave us miracles
in our hearts and lives,
little things that happen
to remind us we're alive.
God gave us the ability
to face each new day
with courage, wisdom,
and a smile from knowing
that whatever sorrow or pain we face,
He abides with us
securely in our hearts.

Most of all, God gave us one another
to teach us about love,
to guide us through this world,
and to help us forward
toward a greater understanding
and a greater sharing and giving
of love.
— Regina Hill

There's an Angel
on Your Shoulder

Have you ever felt that inner tug
        or a silent voice of caution
            or an invisible hand
                leading you down some new path?
Has the light of an exciting new idea
        suddenly lit up in your mind,
            or has an inner sense of love made you
                rise up to help someone in need?
If you look closely you might just see
        an angel sitting on your shoulder!
This heavenly messenger is your own
        personal guardian sent to keep you safe
            and lead you down the steep paths of life.
Your angel will direct your steps
        and watch over you.
Don't worry. Don't give up.
        Just turn your head,
            and you will see your newest friend
                sitting on your shoulder...
        making sure everything is okay!

                            — Dan Lynch

Let Your Spirit Shine Through!

You have an inner jewel. Let your spirit, the divine gem, shine through and create a radiance about you wherever you go.

Let your mind be planted with seeds of love and joy and hope, and courage and universal goodwill and opulent harvest shall grow.

Think of each year as a sower
scattering these seeds in your heart;
then water them with the dews of
sympathy, and throw open the
windows to the broad sunlight of
heaven while they ripen.

And — as surely as the days come and
go — so surely shall your life grow.

— Ella Wheeler Wilcox

May God's Love
Remind You of How
Special You Are

May God's constant love and presence
be near you today and always.
May His warmth brighten your day;
His joy renew your spirit;
His beauty lighten your life;
His assurance give you peace;
His comfort guide you;
His strength empower you;
and His love remind you
just how special you really are.

— Linda E. Knight

What It Means
to Have the Lord
in Your Life

Having the Lord in your life means that you have peace and comfort in your heart as you walk down any pathway your life has to offer.

It means you can pray to a caring and compassionate Father who always has the time to listen and who never fails to understand the hurts and fears that are dwelling in the depths of your soul.

It means having the assurance that nothing can ever come your way that you and He, united together, cannot deal with and ultimately overcome. Even though tears, hurts, and painful times have come and undoubtedly will continue to come, you can know that He has His hand in everything, and things will always work out for your good.

Having the Lord in your life means that you can be assured, with no uncertainty, that you will be given the strength to endure anything that happens to you, and you will become a better person.

Even though all of these blessings are crucial to our day-to-day existence on this earth, they are small compared to the promise of spending an eternity in His presence.

Therefore, what it means to have the Lord in your life is knowing the blessed hope of tomorrow and the glorious promise of heaven that He has prepared for us!

— Cathy Beddow Keener

What Is Faith?

Faith isn't anything you can see;
it isn't anything you can touch.
But you can feel it in your heart.
Faith is what keeps you trying
when others would have given up.
It keeps you believing in
the goodness of others
and helps you find it.
Faith is trusting in a power
greater than yourself
and knowing that whatever happens,
this power will carry you through anything.
It is believing in yourself
and having the courage
to stand up for what you believe in.
Faith is peace in the midst of a storm,
determination in the midst of adversity,
and safety in the midst of trouble.
For nothing can touch a soul
that is protected by faith.

— Barbara Cage

Three Qualities of
a Faith-Filled Life

Transformation

Life has the potential for endless change
and growth — and faith and hope are always
available to guide you. Remember that life has
its cycles just like the seasons, that success
is planted like a seed in every failure, and that
within every ending is a new beginning.

Sacrifice

Achieving your greatest dreams and highest
ideals may call upon you to sacrifice your time,
your talents, and sometimes even your way of
looking at the world. Weigh these sacrifices
carefully; if the reward is worth the effort, go
after it wholeheartedly. However it turns out,
never regret the investments you make in your
dreams. Something good will always come
of them.

And most of all...

Love

Have love not only for others, but for
yourself as well. As a gift, compassion is
one of the best and most widely needed
in the world. Remember that love has the
power to create and sustain life, dreams,
and happiness; it forgives everything and
remembers nothing except the best; and it
lasts forever.

— Edmund O'Neill

Hold On to Hope

What would this world be without Hope? It is the light in the darkness, joy in sorrow, and strength in weakness; without it, the world would be desolate indeed. Its beams are like a great searchlight shining in our hearts, and brightening up every corner, until we mount, as with wings, over difficulties and circumstances, and triumph glorious over the enemy, Despair....

Hold on to the hand of Hope; look into her happy face; catch the inspiration of her smile and the sweetness of her song. Keep trusting and praying, and looking on and up! The bow of promise in God's sky has never failed yet.

— Ida Scott Taylor

As Long as You
Look to the Lord...

You can have hope. Because it works wonders for those who have it. You can be optimistic. Because every cloud does seem to have a silver lining. You can put things in perspective. Because some things are important, and others are not. You can remember that beyond the clouds, the sun is up there shining. You can meet each challenge and give it all you've got.

You can count your blessings. You can be inspired to climb your ladder to the stars. You can be strong and patient. You can be gentle and wise. You can believe in happy endings. Because you are the author of your stories, you can make them turn out the way you want them to. You can bring yourself brighter days.

And you can make your dreams... come true.

— Collin McCarty

The Power of Daily Prayer

A breath of prayer in the morning
   Means a day of blessing sure;
A breath of prayer in the evening
   Means a night of rest secure.

A breath of prayer in our weakness
   Means the clasp of a mighty hand;
A breath of prayer when we're lonely
   Means Someone to understand.

A breath of prayer in rejoicing
   Gives joy and added delight,
For they that remember God's goodness
   Go singing far into the night.

There's never a year nor a season
   That prayer may not bless every hour,
And never a soul need be helpless
   When linked with God's infinite power.

— Frances McKinnon Morton

Prayer is so simple.
It is like quietly opening a door
and slipping into
the very presence of God.
There, in the stillness,
to listen for His voice,
perhaps in petition,
or only to listen,
it matters not.
Just to be there,
in His presence,
is prayer.

— Author Unknown

Prayer is not an act of worship merely, the bending of the knee on set occasions, and offering petitions in need. It is an attitude of soul, opening the life on the Godward side, and keeping free communication with the world of spirit.

— Hugh Black

More things are wrought by prayer than this world dreams of.

— Alfred, Lord Tennyson

God Knows...

When you are tired
and discouraged from
fruitless efforts,
God knows how hard
you have tried.
When you've cried so long
and your heart is in anguish,
God has counted your tears.
If you feel that your life
is on hold
and time has passed you by,
God is waiting with you.
When you're lonely
and your friends are too busy
even for a phone call,
God is by your side...

When you think you've tried everything
and don't know where to turn,
God has a solution.
When nothing makes sense
and you are confused
or frustrated,
God has the answer.
If suddenly your outlook is brighter
and you find traces of hope,
God has whispered to you.
When things are going well
and you have much to be
thankful for,
God has blessed you.

When something joyful happens
and you are filled with awe,
God has smiled upon you.
When you have a purpose to fulfill
and a dream to follow,
God has opened your eyes
and called you by name.
Remember that wherever you are
or whatever you're facing,
God knows.

— Kelly D. Williams

Let God Help

He has helped so many through
    so much.
And He will be there for you
    in your most personal moments
    and through all the times of your life,
        whether they are troubled
            or triumphant.

Take comfort in that thought.
Hold it inside you
    this day and all the days
        of your life.

— Alin Austin

What God
Has Promised

God has not promised
Skies always blue,
Flower-strewn pathways
All our lives through;
God has not promised
Sun without rain,
Joy without sorrow,
Peace without pain.

But God has promised
Strength for the day,
Rest for the labor,
Light for the way,
Grace for the trials,
Help from above,
Unfailing sympathy,
Undying love.

— Annie Johnson Flint

God's Blessings
Are Ours to Cherish

There is so much to be thankful for
    in this world —
the love of our family,
a warm home, good friends,
our health and happiness,
the beauty that surrounds us.

Yet when things aren't going our way,
when sorrow enters our lives
or dreams seem out of reach,
we too quickly forget how fortunate
    we really are.

When difficulties occur,
we must learn to rise above the
feelings of sadness and despair.
We must accept the wisdom of God's plan
and go on with our lives,
grateful for His many blessings,
secure in His embrace.

    — Anna Marie Edwards

Give Thanks
Every Day

Give thanks to God
  And humbly pray
To serve Him well
  This newborn day.

Give thanks to God
  For friends and flowers,
For sunny days
  And cooling showers.

Give thanks to God,
  Fill well your part;
Let love divine
  Possess your heart.

Give thanks to God,
  His bounty see;
Be still and know,
  And grateful be.

— Grenville Kleiser

Would you know who is the greatest Saint in the world: It is not he who *prays* most, or *fasts* most; it is not he who gives most *alms*, or is most eminent for temperance, chastity, or justice; but it is he who is *always thankful* to God, who *wills* everything that God *willeth*, who receives everything as an instance of God's goodness, and has a heart always ready to praise God for it.

— William Law

Lord, Show Us the Way

Oh, Lord, please help to make this day
and all that follow a time of comfort
and understanding.

Please help the light of serenity shine in
through an open door, warming the heart
and encouraging the soul of somebody
who lovingly needs to know... that they are
dearly thought of and cared for, and that
someone is always there for them.

Please help to chase away any clouds and
lessen any troubles in this day.

Please help to provide the reassurance that
hope, blessings, and a world of beautiful
things are always there if we just take the
time to see...

Please help us learn that life goes on, rainbows
   return, and the difficulties that inevitably come
   to everyone turn into insurmountable concerns
   only if we let them.

Please help us realize that problems can only
   impact us to the extent that we give them power
   over our hearts and minds.

Please empower us with patience, faith, and love.

Please help us choose the path we walk instead of
   letting it choose us.

Please let it take us to the brighter day that is
   always there, even though it is not always seen.

Please help us to be wiser than our worries,
    stronger than any situation that can come our
    way, and steadily assured of our beliefs.

Please help us reach the goals that wait for us on
    the horizons that encourage us.

Please enfold us within each new sunset and
    inspire us with each new dawn.

Please help someone who is so deserving of every
    goodness and kindness life can bring.

Please, Lord, help to show the way.

— Douglas Pagels

God Is Love

God is love; His mercy brightens
   All the path in which we rove;
Bliss He wakes and woe He lightens;
   God is wisdom, God is love.

Chance and change are busy ever;
   Man decays, and ages move;
But His mercy waneth never;
   God is wisdom, God is love.

E'en the hour that darkest seemeth,
   Will His changeless goodness prove;
From the gloom His brightness streameth,
   God is wisdom, God is love.

He with earthly cares entwineth
   Hope and comfort from above;
Everywhere His glory shineth;
   God is wisdom, God is love.

— John Bowring

Always remember
that God is not like us.
He is wondrous, amazing,
and beyond our capability
to comprehend.

God is not judgmental —
He understands the motivations
behind your choices and actions,
and His compassion is boundless.
God knows every inch of your being.
He loves all the good things about you,
and He freely forgives you
for your flaws and mistakes.

God knows intimately that you are
like no other person on earth,
and He loves you uniquely.

God is light and life and joy.
He is evident in every smile
that crosses your face.
God is always with you —
supporting you, blessing you,
teaching you, and above all loving you
with a love beyond human understanding.

— Selina Maybury

Anything Is Possible
Because of God

It is God who enables you
to smile in spite of tears;
to carry on when you feel like giving in;
to pray when you're at a loss for words;
to love even though your heart has been
    broken time and time again;
to sit calmly when you feel like throwing
    your hands up in frustration;
to be understanding when nothing
    seems to make sense;
to listen when you'd really rather not hear;
to share your feelings with others
    because sharing is necessary
        to ease the load.

Anything is possible
because God makes it so.

— Faye Sweeney

Everything Happens
for a Reason

Often, it is through
the most difficult days of our lives
that we come to know ourselves
and what is truly most important to us.
No matter how sad you may feel at times,
be confident that hope will
awaken with you tomorrow.
Faith and courage reach out to you;
take hold of them, and you will find
that you will be able to smile again
and truly be happy once more.

How we deal with life
is really a matter of personal choice,
so choose to be happy.
Find joy in the simplest things,
and see beauty in each person you meet.
When times are difficult,
remind yourself that no pain
comes to you without a purpose.
Above all, trust in
God's handcrafted plan
that He has made just for you.
Let Him love you through life's
joyous and painful aspects;
if you do,
you will find inner peace
and unending joy.

— Kelly Wolfe

When One Door
Closes in Our Lives,
God Always Opens Another

Sometimes when we least expect it,
a door closes in our lives.
Circumstances may change,
dreams may get shattered,
and plans for tomorrow may disappear.
But when one door closes,
God always opens another.

When we're facing disappointment
   in our lives,
sometimes it's hard to see
that this is also part of God's plan —
but it's true.
God knows what is best for us,
and He will lead us
to where we need to be.

Have faith in Him, and you will reach
all the wondrous things
that He has waiting for you.

— B. L. McDaniel

Keep up a brave spirit; things are never quite so bad as we imagine they may be. God always lets in the sunshine somewhere. Hope on; no matter how dark the way seems, it is better farther on. Do not be discouraged; if business is dull, if troubles overwhelm you, if you have losses and crosses, or if you are deceived and disappointed, go on hoping and trusting; there is a good time coming for you! Take hold of the everyday duties, and if they are not to your taste, and of your seeking, honor them, anyway. By doing these things well, you shall be found worthy of greater ones. Work and hope; your Better Day will dawn.

— Ida Scott Taylor

There's a light inside you
that is brighter than sunshine.
There's a hope inside you
that can get you through anything.
There's a strength inside you
that is so great that
whatever comes your way today,
you can face it —
with heart, courage, and love.

— Ashley Rice

Do Your Best
...and Leave the Rest to God

Find your strength. Search for that smile of yours that makes everything brighter. Hang in there, even though that can be easier said than done. Have faith.

Don't give up. Make a commitment... between your determination, your hopes, and your heart... that your sun *is* going to shine in the sky. Live your life a day at a time, and things will get better by and by.

Find your way through the days with the light that shines within you. Leave a smile where there wasn't one before. Help a hurt; make it mend. Find the strength to make things right again...

Go forward, from one steppingstone to another. Reach out a little farther. If you believe you can, then you *will* make it through. Listen a little more often to what your heart has to say. Do the things that are important to you.

Make today everything you dreamed it could be. Don't settle for less; don't accept what you should not. Use the precious hours you've been given as wisely as you can. Then do your best, and leave the rest to God.

— Chris Gallatin

He gives strength to the weary and increases the power of the weak. Even youths grow tired and weary, and young men stumble and fall; but those who hope in the Lord will renew their strength. They will soar on wings like eagles; they will run and not grow weary, they will walk and not be faint.

— Isaiah 40:29-31 (NIV)

You'll Never Walk Alone

Sometimes life sends us
changes we've never contemplated,
problems we'd just as soon do without,
and inconveniences that we'd rather not
    have to deal with.
It can feel as if we are wandering
    in a barren desert.

It's during these "desert" experiences
    of our lives
that God, in all His faithfulness,
    opens up His heart.

He quenches our thirsty souls,
revives our parched hearts,
and leads us to a higher place
where peace and joy and love
    will be ours forever.

On all the long journeys
your life leads you on,
please remember...
    you'll never walk alone.

— Linda E. Knight

The Search for God

I took a day to search for God,
And found Him not. But as I trod
    By rocky ledge, through woods untamed,
    Just where one scarlet lily flamed,
I saw His footprint in the sod.

Then suddenly, all unaware,
Far off in the deep shadows, where
    A solitary hermit thrush
    Sang through the holy twilight hush —
I heard His voice upon the air.

And even as I marveled how
God gives us Heaven here and now,
    In a stir of wind that hardly shook
    The poplar leaves beside the brook —
His hand was light upon my brow.

At last with evening as I turned
Homeward, and thought what I had learned
    And all that there was still to probe —
    I caught the glory of His robe
Where the last fires of sunset burned.

Back to the world with quickening start
I looked and longed for any part
    In making saving Beauty be…
    And from that kindling ecstasy
I knew God dwelt within my heart.

— Bliss Carman

You Can Find God Anywhere

God isn't far away;
He surrounds you
with His love.
It was He who opened
your eyes this morning.
It is His strength
that will carry you
through this day,
and it is in His peace
that your heart will
find rest tonight...

God is the light of this day.
He is the sky above you,
the earth beneath you,
and the life of every living thing.

He is in every smile,
in every thought that gives you hope,
in every tear that waters your soul,
and in every moment you can't
face alone.

He's the love on your loved one's face.
He's in the friends along the way —
in strangers you have yet to meet
and blessings you have yet to receive.

He's in every good thing
that touches you.
He is in every step you make
and every breath you take.

— Nancye Sims

God's Promise
to One and All

"I am always with you."
This is the promise of God to one and all —
to every heart that's hurting, grieving,
or burdened with pain.
He offers hope and comfort.
He offers caring and companionship.
He offers peace of mind.
God didn't say the sun would always shine
upon each day.
He didn't say the flowers would always bloom.
He didn't say time would always bring us
perfect happiness.
But God gave humanity a place to go —
a place where peace is always offered,
comfort is always given,
and love is a constant thing.
God said, "I am always with you,"
and He always is.
— Barbara J. Hall

Look at the sky,
and in its vastness
see the love God has for you.
Feel the wind,
and recognize God's touch.

Be aware of the gifts God has given you
every time you feel the connection
you share with family and friends.
Know that He placed them
in your life to fill it
with love you can touch.

Understand that the harder times
are just the uphill parts
of the path God has laid for you,
and if you follow the way faithfully,
He will lead you on
to places of peace and joy.

God surrounds us all the time.
He is in the bad things
as He is in the good things.
Always strive to recognize God
in everything around you.

— Selina Maybury

God Is Lighting
the Way

You are not alone. You never have been, and you never will be. God has been with you every step of the way. Where the path leads, He is lighting lamps to guide you.

And if you ever do feel for a second that He is not right there beside you, it is only because He has gone ahead for a moment or two to build a bridge that will keep you safe from harm and that will lead you on toward the sunlight shining through.

Wherever you go, may you be with God, for God will always be with you.

— Alin Austin

May You Feel God's Presence Every Day

"He Himself has said,
I will not in any way fail you
nor give you up
nor leave you without support."

Hebrews 13:5 (AMP)

May your heart
find peace and comfort in the knowledge
that you are never alone.
May God's presence ease your spirit
and give you rest when you need it.
He knows how you feel.
He is ever aware of your circumstances
and ready to be your strength,
your grace, and your peace.

He is there to cast sunlight
into all of your darkened shadows,
to send encouragement through the love
of friends and family, and
to replace your weariness with new hope.
God is your stronghold,
and with Him as your guide,
you need never be afraid.
No circumstances can block His love.
No grief is too hard for Him to bear.
No task is too difficult
for Him to complete.
When what you are feeling
is simply too deep for words
and nothing anyone does or says
can provide you with the relief you need,
God understands.
He is your provider —
today, tomorrow, and always.
And He loves you.
Cast all of your cares on Him…
    and believe.

— Linda E. Knight

God Is Always
by Your Side

When we are hurting,
God doesn't stay on high.
He brings His majesty to earth
on the wings of love.
When we encounter trials and tribulations,
it is God who will help us face whatever
     is happening in our hearts.
He pours His peace into the moments,
holds our hands, and calms our fears.
He walks with us and talks with us
     along the way.
When we need the ultimate
     in compassion —
the greatest caring, true concern —
it is God's love that wipes each tear away
and brings tomorrow's hope.

God isn't far away...
     He's always by your side.

— Barbara J. Hall

Blue Mountain Arts®

New and Best-Selling Titles

By Susan Polis Schutz:
To My Daughter with Love on the Important Things in Life
To My Son with Love

By Douglas Pagels:
Always Remember How Special You Are to Me
Required Reading for All Teenagers
The Next Chapter of Your Life
You Are One Amazing Lady

By Marci:
Angels Are Everywhere!
Friends Are Forever
10 Simple Things to Remember
To My Daughter
To My Granddaughter
To My Mother
To My Son
You Are My "Once in a Lifetime"

By Wally Amos, with Stu Glauberman:
The Path to Success Is Paved with Positive Thinking

By Minx Boren:
Friendship Is a Journey
Healing Is a Journey

By Carol Wiseman:
Emerging from the Heartache of Loss

Anthologies:
A Daybook of Positive Thinking
A Son Is Life's Greatest Gift
Dream Big, Stay Positive, and Believe in Yourself
Girlfriends Are the Best Friends of All
God Is Always Watching Over You
The Love Between a Mother and Daughter Is Forever
Nothing Fills the Heart with Joy like a Grandson
There Is Nothing Sweeter in Life Than a Granddaughter
There Is So Much to Love About You... Daughter
Think Positive Thoughts Every Day
Words Every Woman Should Remember
You Are Stronger Than You Know